Prayers to My Favorite Saints

REV. LAWRENCE G. LOVASIK, S.V.D.
Divine Word Missionary

PART 1

CONTENTS

Nihil Obstat: Sr. M. Kathleen Flanagan, S.C., Ph.D., Censor Librorum
Imprimatur: ✠ Frank J. Rodimer, J.C.D., Bishop of Paterson

The Nihil Obstat and Imprimatur are official declarations that a book or pamphlet is free of doctrinal or moral error. No implication is contained therein that those who have granted the Nihil Obstat and Imprimatur agree with the contents, opinions or statements expressed.

© 2002 by CATHOLIC BOOK PUBLISHING CORP., Totowa, N.J.
Printed in China   CPSIA   May 2017   10 9 8 7 6 5 4 3 2   L/P
ISBN 978-0-89942-524-5

MARY, MOTHER OF GOD
Queen of All Saints
Died 1st century A.D.   Feast: January 1

MOTHER Mary,
   on this day, I pray
   that you will lovingly watch over me
   as you watched over Jesus.

Please help me
   always to remember
   the special place
   you hold in my life.

Encourage me to trust in you
   when things go wrong
   and turn to you
   when all is well.

Did you know?

Mary's home was Nazareth.

The angel Gabriel visited Mary at the Annunciation.

**Pope Pius XII instituted the Feast of the Queenship
of Mary in 1954.**

SAINT THOMAS AQUINAS
Patron of Catholic Schools
1226 – 1274   Feast: January 28

SAINT Thomas,
I pray that the story of your life
inspires me to do the things
that I am meant to do.

Watch over me
when I am in school
and as I study
while I am at home.

Help me not only to love learning
but also to love and honor our Lord
as deeply as you did.

Did you know?

Saint Thomas was born in Italy.

He joined the Dominicans at age seventeen.

He wrote many books about the teachings of the
Catholic Church.

SAINT BERNADETTE
Lived a Life of Joyful Suffering
1844 – 1879   Feast: February 18

SAINT Bernadette,
 you were just a young girl
 when Our Lady appeared to you,
 but you listened carefully
 to all the Blessed Mother told you.

I ask you to help me
 to pray with all my heart
 for those who suffer.
 May I grow to love the rosary,
 your special prayer to Mary.

Did you know?

Saint Bernadette was born at Lourdes in France.

She first saw Our Lady in 1858.

She joined the Sisters of Charity at Nevers in 1866.

SAINT PATRICK
Patron of Ireland
389 – 461   Feast: March 17

SAINT Patrick,
I pray that I am able
to embrace strangers
with the same love and respect
you showed the Irish.

Please help me to pray often
to all the Persons of the Blessed Trinity,
keeping in mind the image of the shamrock:
three leaves and one stem.

Did you know?

Saint Patrick was born in Scotland.

Pirates captured him when he was sixteen.

He became a Bishop in 432.

SAINT JOSEPH
Patron of the Universal Church
Died 1st century A.D.   Feast: March 19

SAINT Joseph,
   you quietly cared for Jesus and Mary,
   ever mindful of the importance of family.

I pray that I may learn from your example
   so that my love for my family
   grows ever stronger.

Help me to be a person of trust,
   someone who always places faith in God's
   word.

Did you know?

Saint Joseph listened to an angel and fled to Egypt
with Jesus and Mary to keep them safe.

He died in the arms of Jesus and Mary.

He protects all families.

SAINT JOAN OF ARC
Patroness of France
1412 – 1431   Feast: May 30

S AINT Joan,
you were very courageous
as you led soldiers
to defend France against her enemies.

May I be as brave as you
as I live to practice my Faith every day.

You also had a great devotion to the angels.

Help me to pray to my guardian angel
and to seek his protection daily.

Did you know?

Saint Joan was born a peasant.

She led a small army against the enemies of France
at the age of seventeen.

She was burned to death when she was nineteen.

SAINT JOHN THE BAPTIST
Patron of Weavers
Died 1st century A.D.   Feast: June 24

SAINT John,
from the time you were a baby in
your mother's womb,
you knew the joy that only Jesus brings.

Help me to feel that same joy
when I pray to Jesus.

You lived a simple, humble life.

May I never get too caught up in school-
work or play
to show my love for Jesus.

Did you know?

Saint John the Baptist was the cousin of Jesus.

He baptized Jesus at the Jordan River.

King Herod had him beheaded.

SAINT MARIA GORETTI
Patroness of Youth

1890 – 1902   Feast: July 6

✦ ✦ ✦

SAINT Maria,
   you lived a life of goodness and
      obedience,
   and you always kept an open heart.

When others were unkind to you,
   you were loving and forgiving in return.

Please help me to live a life of kindness
   and purity.

May I follow in your footsteps
   and try to live better each and every day.

✦ ✦ ✦

Did you know?

Saint Maria Goretti was born on a small farm
in Italy.

She was a martyr.

Pope Pius XII declared her a Saint in 1950.

SAINT CHRISTOPHER
Patron of Travelers

Died 3rd century A.D.   Feast: July 25

SAINT Christopher,
  you are known to protect people
  when they travel.

Help me to turn to you
    and pray to you
    when my family and I travel
    at special times, like vacation.

But please be with me, too,
    when I travel to and from school,
    to music or sports practice
    or even out for ice cream.

Did you know?

Saint Christopher's name was Offero.

He died a martyr.

He is one of the most popular Saints of the
East and West.

SAINT ROSE OF LIMA
Patroness of South America
1586 – 1617   Feast: August 23

SAINT Rose,
you always thought of other people
and tried to make their lives happier.

May I reach out to others
and show them kindness
even if it is an extra effort for me.

Help me to have a special concern for the
poor,
especially those who are unable
to care for themselves.

Did you know?

Saint Rose was born in Peru in South America.

She offered all her sufferings and good works to
God for sinners.

She is the first Saint of the Americas.

SAINT AUGUSTINE
Patron of Theologians
354 – 430   Feast: August 28

SAINT Augustine,
you did not always live a good life
or choose the best of friends.

When I make mistakes
or join with people who are a bad
influence,
please help me to see what I am doing.

Encourage me to turn away from bad
behavior
and turn toward the way of goodness.

Did you know?

Saint Augustine's mother was Saint Monica.

Saint Ambrose baptized him at the age of
thirty-three.

He was Bishop of Hippo in North Africa for
thirty-five years.

DE
CIVI
TATE
DEI

SAINT THERESA OF THE CHILD JESUS

Patroness of Foreign Missions

1873 – 1897   Feast: October 1

S AINT Theresa,
your life was filled with love for God
and trust in Him,
and you were a very special friend of Jesus.

I pray that you will help me
to follow your example
so that I may grow closer to Jesus.

Please show me how to love
when it is most difficult to show love
to others.

Did you know?

Saint Theresa entered the Carmelite convent at the age of fifteen.

Her "Little Way" means loving and trusting in God as a child.

She is called the Little Flower of Jesus.

SAINT FRANCIS OF ASSISI
Patron of Catholic Action

1181 – 1226   Feast: October 4

SAINT Francis,
you are probably best known
for your love of the poor
and of all God's creatures.

Help me to care for the poor
by small acts of sacrifice.

May I treat those I meet
with kindness,
always remembering
that they are my brothers and sisters.

Did you know?

Saint Francis was a prisoner of war for
almost two years.

He abandoned worldly ways and lived the life
of the poor.

He was the founder of three Franciscan Orders.

SAINT ELIZABETH
Mother of Saint John the Baptist

Died 1st century A.D.   Feast: November 5

SAINT Elizabeth,
you were surprised by the news
that you were to give birth in your
old age.

I pray that I may respond to our God of
surprises
with faith as strong as yours.

May I also be blessed with friends
like the Blessed Mother
who will share the unexpected with me.

Did you know?

Saint Elizabeth was married to Zechariah,
a priest of the Old Law.

She was thought to be unable to have children
because of her advanced age.

She was the cousin of the Blessed Mother.

SAINT NICHOLAS
Patron of Bakers

Born late 3rd century – 342   Feast: December 6

S AINT Nicholas,
   you were a kind and generous man
   and a special friend of children.

I pray that I may always show my gratitude
   to people who are good to me.

May I return their kindness with love
   and may I never hesitate
   to share their care with others.

Did you know?

Saint Nicholas was a monk, an Abbot
and an Archbishop.

The title Santa Claus comes from his name.

The Russian Church honors him more than any
other Saint.

Prayer

T HANK You, God,
for giving me the Saints
as examples of how to live my life.

Day in and day out,
may I turn to them often
to seek encouragement.

I pray that their lives may inspire me
to live a life filled with faith, hope,
and love
and a desire to reach out
to those who may need my help.